Lake District: The **Low Fells**

D1324902

Text: *Steve Goodier and Carl Rogers*
Series editor: *Tony Bowerman*
Photographs: *Carl Rogers, Steve Goodier, Shutterstock, Stewart Smith Photography, Erwin Neudorfer*

Design: *Carl Rogers*

Northern Eye Books

ISBN 978-0-9553557-7-6

A CIP catalogue record for this book is available from the British Library.

www.northerneyebooks.co.uk

Cover: *Catbells (Walk 3)*
Photo: Stewart Smith

First published 2012. This revised edition published in 2019 by:

Northern Eye Books Limited
Northern Eye Books, Tattenhall, Cheshire CH3 9PX
Email: tony@northerneyebooks.com

For sales enquiries, please call 01928 723 744

  @northerneyebooks

 Twitter: @Northerneyeboo

Contents

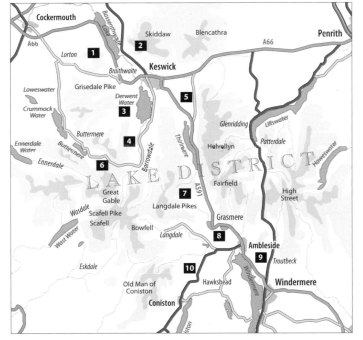

England's Largest National Park

THE LAKE DISTRICT NATIONAL PARK is the largest and most popular of the thirteen National Parks in England and Wales. Created as one of Britain's first National Parks in 1951, its role is to 'conserve and enhance' the natural beauty, wildlife and culture of this iconic English landscape, not just for residents and visitors today but for future generations, too.

Remarkably, the National Park contains every scrap of England's land over 3,000 feet, including its highest mountain, Scafell Pike. Packed within the Park's 885 square miles are numerous peaks and fells, over 400 lakes and tarns, around 50 dales, six National Nature Reserves, and more than 100 Sites of Special Scientific Interest—all publicly accessible on over 1,800 miles of footpaths and other rights of way. It's no surprise then, that the Lake District attracts an estimated 15 million visitors a year.

Panoramic views over Derwent Water from Walla Crag

The Low Fells

The fells get their name from the Old Norse word, *fjalls*, which originally meant areas of rough upland grazing. Today, the Lakeland fells promise some of the best high level walking in England, and a real sense of freedom.

Although the high fells often feature rocky summits, narrow edges and sheer cliffs, the lower fells, below the 2,000 foot contour, are greener, rounder and kinder. Walking on them can still be steep and strenuous, of course, but the routes are more suitable for the general walker. And the views are just as incredible.

"More and more people are turning to the hills; they find something in these wild places that can be found nowhere else."

Alfred Wainwright

TOP 10 **Walks:** The Low Fells

HERE ARE THE TEN MOST POPULAR WALKS on the Lake District's lower fells. Some, like the routes up Catbells, Haystacks or Loughrigg Fell, are timeless classics. Others, like those on Castle Crag and Helm Crag are becoming increasingly well-known. There are routes near busy centres like Ambleside and Keswick, too. But what they all have in common is that they climb to spectacular summits, on clear routes, with marvellous and memorable views.

Lord's Seat & Barf — page 8

Dodd — page 14

Catbells — page 18

Castle Crag — page 24

On the flat summit of Lord's Seat

Lord's Seat & Barf

*Whinlatter Pass Visitor Centre – Lord's Seat – Barf –
Beckstones Gill – Comb Gill – Whinlatter Pass Visitor Centre*

Distance: 8km/ 5 miles

Ascent/descent: 289m/950 feet

Start: Large Pay and Display car park at the Whinlatter Pass Visitor
Centre, near the top of the Whinlatter Pass, west of Braithwaite.
Osprey webcams, café, shop and toilets

Grid ref: NY 208 245

Ordnance Survey Map: OL 4 *The English Lakes North-western area.
Keswick, Cockermouth & Wigton*

Wainwrights: Lord's Seat, Barf

Walk outline

*From the Whinlatter Pass Visitor Centre follow the clearly
waymarked trails into the forest. A circuitous route brings you
out onto the open fell and the summit of Lord's Seat. A good
path continues to the summit of Barf with stunning views over
Bassenthwaite Lake and the distant Skiddaw massif. The route
then crosses Beckstones Gill to rejoin forest tracks and descend
through the trees back to the Whinlatter Pass Visitor Centre.*

Lord's Seat & Barf

The traditional way of climbing these two fells was up
Beckstones Gill from Thornthwaite, but this was often
slippery after rain. Today, better, waymarked paths rise
through Thornthwaite Forest from the Visitor Centre on
the Whinlatter Pass. Walkers can now enjoy these two fells
on good tracks and hill paths. Maps showing the many
waymarked forest trails are available from the visitor centre.

Whinlatter trails

The Whinlatter Forest Park is a real haven for wildlife.
Keep your eyes peeled for red squirrels, roe deer, foxes,
badgers, siskins and crossbills. This is a great fell outing, but
it's worth waiting for a clear day to enjoy the spectacular
views from the top.

Crossbill

0 _____ 1km
_____
½ mile

The Walk

1. Leave the car park and head for the **Whinlatter Pass Visitor Centre**. Immediately to the left of the main entrance, walk through the roofed corridor between the toilets and the gift shop. Out in the open, bear left on the path clearly signed for the 'Walking Trails'.

The waymarked red, blue and green trails all start from this point.

The walk follows part of the green trail signposted for the 'Seat How Summit Trail'. Take the gravel path that bears left into the woods just beyond the sign.

The path climbs past a play area and bends to the right, up through the woods. Keep to the green route at any junctions to reach an open viewpoint and picnic area with low, half-log seats.

A panorama opens out before you. Beyond the broad Derwent valley, the view spans the Helvellyn group, and the Dodds ridge, beyond Keswick. Away to the left, the southern slopes of Skiddaw rise steeply above Bassenthwaite Lake, still hidden from sight below.

Take the path straight ahead from the seats, keeping to the green route and climbing steeply beneath the woodland canopy. Rise to a T-junction where the path meets a broad forest track, and turn left. Follow the track, passing a viewpoint and information panel on your left, and continue as it swings sharply to the right, ignoring any paths off to the left.

The track climbs steadily for about 700 metres before levelling off at a junction of paths beside a turning area.

Wide views: *Looking south to Grisedale Pike and Grasmoor from Lord's Seat*

2. Leave the green route here, which heads off to the right. Instead, follow the forest track straight ahead. The track begins to descend and curves to the right. Follow the track downhill, ignoring minor paths on either side, until you reach a sharp left-hand bend.

3. Leave the main track here, taking a narrow path on the right immediately after the bend; it's marked by a post with the number 24 on it. Follow this path steeply uphill through the woods

to reach a boggy area near the top of the rise. A little farther on, when the path joins a broader track at a T-junction, turn left. Climb on through sparser woodland, now with widening views, until you emerge onto the open hillside. Walk ahead, to cross a stile just before the **summit of Lord's Seat**.

Although the fell itself is nothing special, the 360° panorama from the summit is just superb.

4. Take the grassy path northeast from the top of Lord's Seat, heading for the distant Skiddaw group. Lower down, the

Lakes and fells: *Panoramic view towards Skiddaw and Bassenthwaite from Lord's Seat*

path begins to curve to the right and heads towards Barf. Keep to the right-hand side of the broad, rounded ridge. Walk on, to cross a boggy area where you will have to pick your route carefully in wet conditions. Things improve as you approach the hill, where a short but steep climb takes you up to the **summit of Barf** with its excellent views.

5. Continue over the summit in a southerly direction, heading for distant Keswick. The path soon swings to the right and descends diagonally towards a stile on the edge of the forest below.

6. Cross **Beckstones Gill** and go up the other side to cross the stile. Follow the path ahead to reach a forest track. Turn left here, and follow the track through the woods, descending slightly and passing marker post 21. Continue ahead on the main track, rising to a T-junction marked by two posts, one of them showing the number 8.

7. Turn left at the T-junction, and descend past the green-route marker post number 54. Ignore the path on the right here, and instead continue ahead on the forest track. At the next junction, bear right at post number 9. Stay on this forest track, climbing gently, before

contouring around the hillside to cross a small stream (named **Comb Gill** on larger OS maps). Walk on for around 1.5 kilometres.

8. Immediately after crossing a stream (called **Black Gill** on the map), look out for post 1 on the right, and bear left where the track forks. Follow this track downhill, back to the Visitor Centre and the car park to complete the walk ♦

Red squirrels in Whinlatter Forest

Whinlatter Forest Park is an important red squirrel reserve and one of the best places in England to see these popular yet increasingly rare mammals. The large, mainly coniferous forest is actively managed to provide ideal habitat for them. So far, it seems, the project is paying off: a survey during the summer of 2010 counted more than 400 red squirrels living among the trees.

Dodd rising above Bassenthwaite Lake

A circuit of **Dodd**

Old Sawmill Tearoom car park – Dodd Wood – Long Doors Pass – Dodd – Dodd Wood – Tearoom car park

What to expect:
Clear forest tracks and paths. Some steep ascents and descents

Distance: 5.5km/ 3½ miles

Ascent/descent: 395m/1,300 feet

Start: Forestry Commission Pay and Display car park at the Old Sawmill Tearoom, on the A591 north of Keswick

Grid ref: NY 235 283

Ordnance Survey Map: OL 4 *The English Lakes North-western area. Keswick, Cockermouth & Wigton*

Wainwrights: Dodd

Walk outline

This walk to the top of Dodd uses a combination of waymarked and unmarked forest tracks. The maze of paths can be confusing, so allow plenty of time to complete the circuit. From the Old Sawmill Tearoom, forest tracks lead ever upwards to the saddle of Long Doors, from where a hill path takes you to the summit. A bit of backtracking and careful route-finding are required to find the way down. More forest tracks return you to the picnic areas, toilets, and the Old Sawmill Tearoom and the car park.

Dodd

Until a few years ago, Dodd was smothered in conifers and a trip to the top was a dodgy business involving a push through dense woodland, with scant views as reward for your efforts. Happily, all that has changed. The trees around the summit have been felled, creating a new and stunning panorama.

Dodd Wood also contains two signposted viewpoints where you can watch for red squirrels and the famous Bassenthwaite Lake ospreys. In season, they're staffed by experts with binoculars and high-powered telescopes.

Dodd summit

Trail sign

The Walk

1. From the car park walk past the **Old Sawmill Tearoom** and take the path signed for 'All Trails'. Cross the wooden footbridge, bear right immediately and zig-zag up to join the tarmac path above. Turn right and follow the path uphill for 750 metres, almost ½ mile.

2. At a path junction (footpath left and right), turn right (waymarked for the Red/Green route) and follow the path down to cross a wooden footbridge over the beck. Continue on the path beyond the bridge to reach a T-junction.

Turn sharp left and follow the forest track uphill through **Dodd Wood**. Ignore any side paths or tracks and climb to reach a major junction where another track joins from the left.

Continue on a little further almost to the saddle known as **Long Doors Pass**.

3. Roughly 70 metres after the junction, bear right onto a good path signposted for 'Dodd Summit'. Shortly you reach a viewpoint with a seat and a grand view over the town of Keswick and Derwwent Water. The path turns sharp right here and makes its way above the remaining sections of the forest, passing felled areas and occasional rock outcrops. Stay on the main path, ignoring paths off to either side, and soon the top of the fell comes into view ahead. Follow the good path all the way to the **summit of Dodd.**

4. Leave the summit by the same route retracing your steps for about 450 metres to a path on the right with a marker post for the Green route. Take this path heading for a bench (with Derwent Water in the distance) but turn off the path to the right before you reach the bench.

Follow this path downhill; it soon improves. Keep straight ahead, eventually curving to the right around the slopes of Dodd—with great views of **Bassenthwaite Lake** down to the left and ahead.

The path eventually enters thicker

```
0                          1km
|_____|
|--------------------------|
0                       ½ mile
```

Birds-eye view: *Looking down to Bassenthwaite Lake from the summit of Dodd*

woods Keep ahead until the path bends to the left, and zig zags steeply down to reach a good forest track at a T-junction below.

5. Turn right, downhill on this track, to eventually reach another T-junction.

Turn left here and at the next fork, bear right (marked for the Red/Green route). Continue down to a crosspaths and turn right. Follow the curving path down through the wood. Finally, descend past the footbridge to re-enter the car park at the **Old Sawmill Tearoom**, to complete the walk. ♦

The Bassenthwaite ospreys

Ospreys are large fish-eating birds of prey that breed at only a handful of sites across Britain. They had been absent from England since the 1830s until they returned to an artificial nesting platform at Dodd Wood in 2001. The pair , nicknamed 'No-ring' and 'Mrs', have raised chicks every year since. The ospreys usually return from their African wintering grounds in early April and stay over the summer, leaving in late August.

Looking towards the summit from Skelgill Bank

Catbells

Hawse End – Skelgill Bank – Catbells – Hause Gate – Allerdale Ramble – Hawse End

What to expect:
Good, clear fell paths along a grassy ridge with stunning views

Distance: 6.5km/ 4 miles

Ascent/descent: 380m/1,250 feet

Start: Limited free parking at Hawse End, near Gutherscale Lodge, on the minor road south of Portinscale and Swinside.

Grid ref: NY 247 213

Ordnance Survey Map: OL 4 *The English Lakes North-western area. Keswick, Cockermouth & Wigton*

Wainwrights: Catbells

Walk outline

The roadside parking at Hawse End soon gets congested on fine days. Yet within minutes you leave all that behind and head up the wonderful ridge of Skelgill Bank. It is everything a Lakeland ridge should be with narrow sections and some lovely rocky steps. A superb two kilometre walk brings you to the summit of Catbells. The scenic descent drops to the pass of Hause Gate. From here, a constructed path descends towards Derwent Water with the lake spread out below. Not far from the bottom an excellent track is joined to work an elevated route back to Hawse End.

Summit of Catbells

Catbells

Catbells is not quite as easy as some people think. The Skelgill Bank ridge is a stiff climb and the two main rocky steps—one in the lower reaches and another just below the summit—can be tricky and require care in bad weather.

Even so, the paths are good and the views spectacular, so save this walk for a clear day. Although the summit is often crowded, in the early morning or evening it is a wonderful place to soak up the surroundings, relax and daydream.

Wheatear

The Walk

1. From **Hawse End**, follow the road up to a cattle grid. Just before the grid, bear left through a gate and follow the path ahead, keeping the wire fence to your left. Continue uphill to the road and cross over, bearing half-left, to the broad path opposite.

A little farther on, leave the path, and cut back to the right, to take another steeply rising path. The path climbs steadily, kinks to the left, and continues upwards. Follow the path, which has steps in places, to the ridge end.

The path heads straight up for a while, before zig-zagging more steeply uphill. Occasional fences stop walkers from taking shortcuts and eroding the slopes. Higher up, continue past a path joining from the right that comes up from an alternative parking area below. Continue upwards to the end of **Skelgill Bank**.

2. Continue uphill along the ridge, which gradually becomes more defined. Climb up to a rock step below a memorial plaque. At the top, ascend easily at first and then more steeply along Skelgill Bank. Beyond a minor rocky top, the path continues along the ridge towards the summit of Catbells, now visible ahead.

The name Catbells probably comes from the Cumbrian dialect phrase 'Cat bields', meaning a place where 'wildcats shelter'. There is a place still called Cat Bields on Seatallen fell, near Wasdale.

Beyond a slight rise, the path drops down to a saddle where another path rises to join from the left. The path up the final slopes of Catbells is rough in

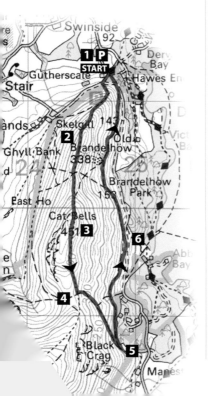

0   1km
⊢——————⊣
½ mile

Long and winding road: *From Catbells the route continues to Hause Gate*

parts. Although it forks occasionally, all routes eventually lead to the summit.

If you fancy more of a scramble to the top, bear left to the crest of the rising ridge, which leads to the base of another rock step. Scramble up and continue to the rocky **summit of Catbells**.

The 360° panorama from the broad, rocky summit is dominated by Derwent Water, far below. To the north are Keswick,

Skiddaw, the Newlands Valley and Bassenthwaite Lake, while to the south is beautiful Borrowdale.

3. Drop south from the summit, descending carefully down a rocky step. Take the good path ahead, towards Maiden Moor. The path descends all the way to a fork just above the saddle of **Hause Gate**.

The old workings, spoil heaps and shafts close to Yewthwaite Gill, on the western side of the ridge below, are the remains of lead mines last worked in the 1890s.

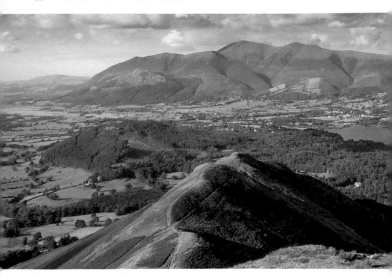

Stunning view: *Catbells enjoys panoramic views across Derwent Water to Keswick*

4. Take the left-hand path here, which descends on a well-constructed route towards Derwent Water, below. The path snakes left and right to drop steeply down the fellside. Continue past an anti-erosion fence for a 100 metres or so, to reach a clear junction of paths.

5. Take the left-hand fork here, and head downhill again, now with the Manesty Park woods below to your right. Continue downhill to join a track alongside a wall on the right. Continue on the track, which rises past the wall.

Nearby is a bench and plaque commemorating the successful nineteenth-century novelist, Sir Hugh Walpole. Brackenburn Lodge, where he lived and worked from 1924 until 1941, overlooks Derwent Water below.

Continue to curve right between fences, with Derwent Water below to the right. The track is part of the long distance **Allerdale Ramble**. The path drops gently to the road below, to emerge at a marker post and a quarry parking area.

6. Take the path ahead that rises from the quarry, leaving the road behind. The path climbs for a while, then levels

where another path joins from the left. The path climbs again before beginning a gradual descent in the direction of Skiddaw, ahead.

Walk on, to rejoin your outward route at the junction for the ridge climb. Descend to the road and cross it to a path opposite. Go through the gate by the cattle grid and return to the parking area to complete the walk. ♦

Fix the Fells

Around 10 million walkers use the Lake District's footpaths each year. Their pounding feet contribute to erosion that can be particularly bad on popular routes. Since 1993, the National Park Authority, National Trust and English Nature have been working together to manage the problem. Key techniques include 'soil inversion', and 'stone pitching': where naturally occurring rocks are dug into the ground to create firm footfalls.

Castle Crag from the path to High Doat

Castle Crag

Rosthwaite – River Derwent – Castle Crag – Tongue Gill – High Doat – Seatoller – River Derwent – Rosthwaite

Distance: 8,5km/ 5¼ miles

Ascent/descent: 275m/900 feet

Start: National Trust Pay and Display car park, west of the Borrowdale Road, at Rosthwaite – signposted from the village. Alternative parking and start at Seatoller (see point 7 on map)

Grid ref: NY 258 149

Ordnance Survey Map: OL 4 *The English Lakes North-western area. Keswick, Cockermouth & Wigton*

Wainwrights: Castle Crag

Walk outline

From Rosthwaite car park, the walk crosses the River Derwent before tackling the rough slopes of Castle Crag. A slippery descent from the summit brings you to a ravine where you join the Allerdale Ramble and follow the trail across open country. Leaving the trail, the route traverses High Doat before following a network of paths to Seatoller, below the Honister Pass. The return to Rosthwaite runs alongside the River Derwent before crossing on stepping stones, or via New Bridge, if the river is high.

Castle Crag

Alfred Wainwright said of Castle Crag, 'If a visitor to Lakeland has only two to three hours to spare, poor fellow, yet desperately wants to reach a summit and take back an enduring memory of the beauty and atmosphere of the district, let him climb Castle Crag'. That sums it up nicely. Despite being only 300 metres high, the climb to the summit has all the drama of the high tops.

Castle Crag dominates the 'Jaws of Borrowdale' and was once topped by a prehistoric hillfort. Today, it's popular with fell walkers, and the home of resident peregrines.

Castle Crag quarry

Peregrine

0   1km

1 mile

The Walk

1. Leave the car park and turn right along the lane. At the end of the lane, walk through the farmyard and continue along a track. The track curves to the [rig]ht and runs alongside the River [Der]went to the stone-built **New Bridge**.

2. Cross the bridge and continue to a T-junction. Turn right, go through a gate, and follow the path alongside the river on a path shared by the **Cumbria Way**.

Beside a small wooded rise, the path swings to the left, away from the river. When it bears right after the trees, cross a stile on the left. The path climbs steeply now and gets rougher, ascending through open woods. Higher up, go through a gap in the wall and continue up the field to cross a stile in the corner. Go right, towards a large cairn below spoil heaps. Bear right, up a constructed path that zig-zags up through the spoil to a flatter area near a quarry on the left. Take the path ahead, to the right of the quarry, to reach the **summit of Castle Crag**.

3. Retrace your steps back to the large cairn below the constructed path. Turn right here to take a rough path that cuts back to the left, zig-zagging steeply downhill to a fence corner. Cross the stile and continue downhill, eventually passing through a gap in the wall. Leave the path when it curves to the right, walking ahead on a grassy path to join a broad stony path. Turn left.

Rocky peak: *Castle Crag with Skiddaw and Derwent Water pale on the horizon*

4. Just over the rise, bear left at a fork off the main path and take a contouring line to cross **Tongue Gill** by a large wooden footbridge. Follow the path to the left through a gate and continue on the good path ahead across the open fell, climbing gently.

Go through a gate, cross a footbridge and continue, soon beside a wall on the left, towards a pass on the skyline ahead. Cross another footbridge just before you reach the pass.

5. Cross the wall on the left by a ladder stile and follow a descending path over boggy ground. Cross a stream and climb steadily to eventually cross a stile in the wall above. The path swings left, and then right, up to the broad **summit of High Doat**. The highest top is the last, unmarked bump on the right.

6. Continue on the main path, dropping to a small valley with woods ahead. At a T-junction, turn right on a path that passes a cairn in a hollow. Continue downhill through a gap in the wall and bear to the right when the path forks

Low fells: *Looking back to Castle Crag and Rosthwaite from the path to High Doat*

Lower down, join a grassy track that bears right to cross a stile beside a gate. Follow the path alongside the wall to a second junction next to a gate on the left. Turn left through the kissing gate, and follow the path as it sweeps to the right past a group of pines. Continue on the track down to a gate onto the road at **Seatoller**.

7. Turn left along the road and walk through Seatoller. Immediately beyond the cottages, turn left into the **National ⸽ ust car park** (alternative parking and ⸽ . Take the track in the far right-hand

corner. Rise to cross a stile by a gate. Bear right by a wall and take the right-hand fork twenty metres later. Stay beside the wall passing the outdoor centre, down to the right. Turn right through a kissing gate in the wall and bear left on an obvious path through the woods. The path passes through several walls, with the river down to the right.

Beyond a kissing gate, the path hugs the river, with a short scramble over rocks. Continue on the good riverside path to the **Youth Hostel**.

8. Pass the Youth Hostel and follow the drive as it curves to the right. Turn left on the signposted path immediately before

the bridge. Follow a farm access road; when this curves left into the farmyard, go through a kissing gate ahead. Follow the riverside path to the **stepping stones**.

9. Cross the river on the stepping stones to pick up your outward route to complete the walk. (Or if the river is high, walk on to cross the river by the **New Bridge**). ♦

Hillforts and Heroes

Castle Crag dominates the strategic 'Jaws of Borrowdale'. Thousands of years ago its small but level summit was the site of an Iron Age hillfort, traces of whose drystone ramparts can still be seen. Today, the much quarried summit hosts a circular slate cairn and poignant memorial to Lieutenant Hamer and the other Borrowdale men who died fighting for their country during the First World War.

The little church of St John's in the Vale and the distant summit of Skiddaw

High Rigg

*St John's in the Vale church – High Rigg – St John's Beck –
Low Bridge End Farm – St John's in the Vale church*

What to expect:
*Clear grassy paths over
the open fell with grand
views*

Distance: 7.5km/ 4½ miles

Ascent/descent: 150m/500 feet

Start: Limited parking near the end of the minor road to the church of St John's In the Vale

Grid ref: NY 306 224

Ordnance Survey Map: OL 5 *The English Lakes North-eastern area.
Penrith, Patterdale & Caldbeck*

Wainwright summits: High Rigg

Walk outline

*From the tiny church of St John's in the Vale, a good path
rises steeply to the summit of High Rigg, where you can
either scramble up the rocks to the top or take an easier route
around the back. From the summit, the path continues along
the broad ridge with superb views. The route traverses rough
ground before descending to St John's Beck. The return path
runs around the eastern side of High Rigg, past tearooms, and
along the edge of the valley of St John's In the Vale.*

High Rigg

The late Alfred Wainwright reckoned that High Rigg could
be climbed in fifteen minutes from the little church of St
John's in the Vale, if you were full of the joys of spring. It
probably can be; but it is far too good a summit to rush
up, and you should take as long as you like to complete
this energetic circuit and traverse the lovely ridge. At
just 357 metres above sea level, High Rigg is no giant
and is surrounded by far higher ground, but it has all the
attributes of a good top: a rocky summit, steepish ascent
and superb views from its upper reaches. Make sure you
save this route for a sunny day to get the very best from it.

Summit of High Rigg

Bilberries

Green lane: *Looking across St John's in the Vale to distant, cloud-capped Blencathra*

The Walk

1. From the parking area near the tiny **church of St John's in the Vale,** begin by taking the path to the right of the Youth Centre buildings. This curves left behind the buildings, then swings to the right, to a kissing gate in the wall. Go through the gate and climb the steeply rising path. Stay with the main path until it reaches level ground and the rocky summit appears ahead.

A straightforward path between swathes of bracken climbs easily to the **summit of High Rigg.** As you approach the summit, scramble up the final rocks to the right, following the obvious route to the highest point. If you don't fancy the scramble, circle around the summit rocks on easier ground.

The summit is little more than the highest point on a broad, knobbly ridge but it is a superb viewpoint. Even its name, Rigg, comes from an Old English word meaning a bumpy fell or ridge. The summit panorama takes in the giants of Skiddaw

*and Blencathra, seen at arm's length
to the north, the broad backs of
the Dodds and the Helvellyn range
close by to the east, and the distant
Derwent Fells beyond Keswick
out to the west. To the south you
can see Thirlmere surrounded by
woods and the distant gap of
Dunmail Raise.*

2. Head south from the summit
on a good path over the open,
grassy fell. At a fork, go left to
a wall ahead. Follow the path
beside the wall on the right-hand
side, at one point curving to the right,
away from the wall, to avoid boggy
ground. Rejoin the wall and follow the
path ahead past outcrops and over
broken ground, eventually descending
to a stile in a wall corner.

3. Cross the stile and walk ahead to a
fork in the path. Bear right here (on the
path ahead), continuing on the main
path with higher ground up to the left.

The path traces the contours, sweeping
to the left, to cross a stile in a fence.
The grassy path continues along
the narrowing ridge, and eventually
descends through rocks to go through
a gap in the wall. A final ascent leads to
pine trees framing a view of Helvellyn,
then drops through open woods on an
obvious path.

0   1km
                    1 mile

St John's in the Vale: *High Rigg enjoys superb views in all directions , especially north into St John's in the Vale and across to Great Dodd and Watson's Dodd, with Blencathra in the distance*

The path levels before a final descent to a path T-junction. Turn left here to reach the path above **St. John's Beck**.

4. Follow the path through woods with the beck down to the right.

Finally, descend to the river and follow the path through an area of rocks to reach an old wall on the right. The path continues beside the wall to a gate and

stile close to **Low Bridge End Farm**. The tearoom here is a good place for a break. There is a camping barn here, too. Cross the stile and head to the left of the farm and tearoom, on a path signposted 'To the Church'.

5. Pass to the left of farm buildings and continue on the path beside a wall on the right. The path soon enters the lower edge of woods. Walk on beside the wall.

When the trees end, continue between mossy walls with the open fell up to the left. The good path rises slightly after a gate, with fields on the right.

There are grand views up the valley to the

south face of Blencathra seen across the level fields of St John's in the Vale.

6. Finally, climb steeply to cross a stile beside a gate that leads out into a lane.

Turn left up the lane. Walk on, past the church of **St John's in the Vale**, to complete the walk. ◆

The church of St John's in the Vale

High on the valley's western flank is the tiny stone church of St John's in the Vale. It sits on an ancient track over the hills between Matterdale and Wanthwaite. Although the present building dates from 1845, there may have been a church here centuries earlier. Local legend suggests the Vale is named after the Knights Hospitallers of the Order of St. John of Jerusalem, who are said to have built a chapel in the valley back in the thirteenth century.

Haystacks from Gatesgarth

Haystacks

Gatesgarth – Warnscale Beck – Dubs Quarry – Innominate Tarn – Haystacks – Scarth Gap – Gatesgarth

What to expect:
Rocky fell paths that are confusing in poor visibility. Steep descent

Distance: 7.25km/ 4½ miles

Ascent/descent: 655m/2,150 feet

Start: Car park (small fee) at Gatesgarth Farm at the foot of the Honister Pass, on the Buttermere side. Often busy

Grid ref: NY 194 149

Ordnance Survey Map: OL 4 *The English Lakes North-western area. Keswick, Cockermouth & Wigton*

Wainwrights: Haystacks

Walk outline

From the car park at Gatesgarth Farm a good, well-used path leads up through the atmospheric amphitheatre of Warnscale Bottom. Higher up a steep rocky path climbs beside Warnscale Beck to reach, first Blackbeck Tarn, then the famous Innominate Tarn. The path continues to Haystacks summit with superb views. A very rough descent with a little scrambling brings you to the pass of Scarth Gap. From here a good path drops back to the shores of Buttermere with an easy walk back across the flat meadows to the car park.

Haystacks

This is a wonderful little fell hiding itself amongst the giants of the central fells at the head of Buttermere. The fact that it doesn't quite reach 2,000 feet has not prevented it from becoming one of the most popular fells in the Lake District. A true miniature mountain, its summit is wild and rocky with magnificent views down into Buttermere and Ennerdale.

The name Haystacks comes from the old Norse word stack, meaning 'a column-like rock'. Wainwright preferred the simpler translation 'High Rocks'.

Haystacks summit

Raven

The Walk

1. Turn left out of the car park and walk along the road towards the Honister Pass. Around 200 metres later, take the broad track/path on the right, directly below the imposing north ridge of Fleetwith Pike. The track skirts around the base of the fell with walled pastures to the right.

2. As the path begins to climb, ignore the path forking off to the right, staying with the main path beside **Warnscale Beck**. Further up, the path zigzags, then turns sharp left at a point where the beck flows through a ravine below.

Higher up, the angle eases and ahead there are areas of spoil associated with **Dubs Quarry**. Just before you reach the quarry area and the stone quarry house of 'Dubs Bothy', bear right and cross the beck.

3. The well-used path leads ahead, passing close to the knobbly crag of **Little Round How**. Continuing ahead, the path crosses the stream flowing out of **Blackbeck Tarn**.

The path climbs over rough ground, and fords a second stream to reach the superbly positioned **Innominate Tarn**, with its wide, mountain views.

4. A clear path continues past the tarn and on to the **summit of Haystacks**— a rocky ridge with a cairn at either end. The left-hand cairn, as you approach, is the higher of the two and the true summit of the fell.

5. From the summit, walk along the rocky ridge to the second cairn. Go left, dropping to go to the right of a small pool and pass over a rocky rib. Now descend the rough path, passing carefully down rocky steps. Go right of a fence end to reach a junction of paths with a large cairn at **Scarth Gap**.

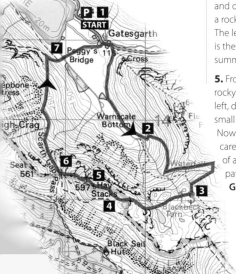

0   1km

1 mile

Mountain high: *Walkers on the summit*

6. Take the path to the right here, towards Buttermere. The path is wide and unmistakable, with the lake ahead. Lower down, go through a gap in the wall and continue to descend until you reach a small wood on the right. Turn sharp right immediately beyond the wood, descending to pass through a kissing gate to reach a farm track.

7. Cross the footbridge over **Warnscale Beck** and follow the path towards **Gatesgarth Farm**. Pass through a kissing gate to the right of the farm and turn left to return to the car park to complete the walk. ♦

Wainwright Heaven?

Haystacks was the favourite fell of the celebrated Lake District guidebook writer, Alfred Wainwright. In 'The Pictorial Guide to the Lakeland Fells', he wrote that 'for beauty, variety and interesting detail ... the summit area of Haystacks is supreme. This is, in fact, the best fell-top of all.' When he died in 1991, his wife carried his ashes to the summit and scattered them near Innominate Tarn.

Helm Crag from the southeast ridge of Steel Fell

Helm Crag

Greenburn – Green Burn – Helm Crag – Gibson Knott – Calf Crag – Steel Fell – Greenburn

What to expect:
Fell paths, wet and boggy in places with a steep ascent/descent

Distance: 9.5km/ 6 miles

Ascent/descent: 700m/2,300 feet

Start: Limited parking near Raise Beck on the minor road north of Grasmere, west of the A591, near Ghyll Foot Farm

Grid ref: NY 332 096

Ordnance Survey Map: OL 5 *The English Lakes North-eastern area. Penrith, Patterdale & Caldbeck*

Wainwrights: Helm Crag, Calf Crag, Steel Fell

Walk outline

The route heads up the glacial valley of Greenburn beside the aptly named Green Burn. Across the burn, a steep path takes you to the ridge above—where an out-and-back route visits the summit of Helm Crag. A lovely ridge walk follows, with the path climbing over Gibson Knott to the end of the ridge at Calf Crag. From there, the route circles the head of Greenburn, passing the high-level Steel Fell Tarn to climb to the final summit—Steel Fell. The final section is a descent of the dramatic southeast ridge of Steel Fell.

Ascending Helm Crag

Helm Crag

Helm Crag is a must for all fell wanderers, but the popular route is always busy. The walk described here avoids the crowds by climbing up from Greenburn. The Helm Crag to Calf Crag ridge is a real gem and gives a dramatic walk unique among Lakeland's lower fells. Both Gibson Knott and Calf Crag are great tops with stunning views from their upper reaches. The circuit around Greenburn Head and Steel Fell provides dramatic views of Thirlmere and the final descent down Steel Fell's southeast ridge is a great way to end any Lakeland day.

Cotton grass

The Walk

1. From the parking area close to **Raise Beck**, walk back along the lane. Cross the bridge and turn right up an access lane just before the buildings of **Ghyll Foot Farm**. The lane eventually ends by a cottage and large house. Go through the gate on the left and take the lower, left-hand path on the right, which heads up the Greenburn valley. Beyond a gate, drop down to the left to a wooden footbridge over **Green Burn**.

2. Over the bridge, take the steep, grassy path ahead. Go through a kissing gate at the top of the field and then through the left-hand of two gaps in the wall opposite. The path continues steeply uphill. Beyond a gap in a crossing wall, take the zig-zagging path up to the ridge at **Bracken Hause**. Turn left on a good path to the **summit of Helm Crag**.

The true summit is actually the top of the rock outcrop known as the 'Howitzer', but most people are content not to reach it! In fact, it's the only Wainwright summit that Wainwright never reached.

3. Retrace your steps back to **Bracken Hause** and continue on the good path along the ridge. The path crosses craggy

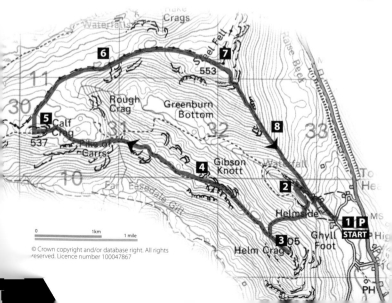

Rocky pinnacle: *The rock known as 'The Howitzer' is the highest point on Helm Crag*

ground, eventually rising to the cairn on the **summit of Gibson Knott**.

4. Continue along the ridge over rough ground towards Calf Crag, ahead. In about a kilometre the path reaches two cairns at a small saddle before the final rise. Continue over rocky ground between small crags. The path then crosses flatter, wetter ground to arrive at the rock outcrop on the **summit of Calf Crag**.

5. From the summit, turn north (right as you approached), keeping to the right of an outcrop a few metres from the summit. The faint path soon improves. Descend over wet ground around the head of Greenburn Bottom, to your right. At a line of old fence posts, the path swings east along the wide ridge. Follow the fence posts to Steel Fell Tarn (there are actually two tarns here).

6. Walk on along the wide ridge using the old fence line as a guide. Stick to the main path as it climbs steadily, ignoring minor side paths.

Glacial valley: *The view down Greenburn Bottom to Helm Crag from the broad ridge below Calf Crag*

From this broad ridge you have a good view into Greenburn Bottom, a classic example of a post glacial valley. This was carved by one of the numerous glacial tongues that flowed from an icecap centred over Esk Hause.

Greenburn Bottom is typical of a Lakeland dale and displays the classic 'U' shape. The hummocky mounds that litter the floor of the valley are composed of the rock and ꜜild debris transported and deposited by ꜜlacier.

When you reach an intact fence on the left, follow it up steeper ground to the **summit of Steel Fell**.

7. From the summit, take the faint path south-east to join a better path coming in from the east cairn. Bear right here, and follow the good path down the lovely **southeast ridge of Steel Fell**. The path skirts to the left twice to avoid crags but remains distinct. After the second outcrop you reach a kissing gate in a wall.

8. Pass through the kissing gate and follow a wall on your right. Cross an old wall at a gap, walk on to a field corner

and go through a gate. Now go half-left on the path, pass through a gap in the wall and continue downhill to rejoin the Greenburn path from the outward journey.

Follow this down to the gate at the head of the access road used at the start of the walk. Retrace your outward journey to complete the walk. ♦

'The Lion and the Lamb'

Helm Crag was a favourite fell of both Wordsworth and Wainwright. Each of them mentions the upright rocks at either end of the ridge. The higher, north-western outcrop is known as the 'Howitzer', while the southern outcrop, visible from Grasmere, is called the 'Lion and the Lamb'. Inspired by these curiously-shaped rocks, Wordsworth wrote: ' Dread pair that, spite of wind and weather, Still sit on Helm Crag together'.

Looking down to Grasmere from Loughrigg Fell

Loughrigg Fell

*Rydal – Loughrigg Terrace – Loughrigg Fell – Lily Tarn –
River Rothay – Rydal Park – Rydal*

What to expect:
*Clear well used tracks on
lower ground, open fell
paths, one steep ascent*

Distance: 11.5km/ 7 miles

Ascent/descent: 533m/1,750 feet

Start: Small car park over the stone bridge, just off the A591,
immediately before Rydal (approaching from Ambleside)

Grid ref: NY 364 060

Ordnance Survey Map: OL 7 *The English Lakes South-eastern area
Windermere, Kendal & Silverdale*

Wainwrights: Loughrigg Fell

Walk outline

*The route begins in the hamlet of Rydal and climbs gently
across the lower slopes of Loughrigg Fell above Rydal Water
and Grasmere. A steep fell path then climbs to the summit
where views open out in all directions—north across Grasmere
and Rydal Water and south to Elter Water and the distant
Windermere. A maze of narrow paths head across the open fell
to the tiny Lily Tarn, then down towards Ambleside. The return
to Rydal is through the parkland of Rydal Hall.*

Loughrigg

Loughrigg is a fell that doesn't grab the eye—it lacks the
iconic profile of Helm Crag or Catbells, but is in a great
location with superb views in every direction. There is
water on three sides, with Grasmere and Rydal Water to
the north, Windermere to the south, and Loughrigg Tarn
and Elter Water to the southwest. And the fells of southern
Lakeland are arranged around it in an impressive arc—from
the Kentmere fells in the east, past Red Screes, the Fairfield
Horseshoe, High Raise and the Langdale fells, to the Coniston fells out to the southwest. What's more, you can enjoy
a bird's-eye view of Ambleside towards the end of the walk.

Grasmere from Loughrigg

Meadow pipit

The Walk

1. Turn left out of the car park and walk along the rising lane. At the end of the tarmac the lane continues as a rough track between stone walls. Go through a gate where the path forks and continue on the path ahead, high above **Rydal Water**, with views across to Nab Scar.

2. Soon the path zig-zags up to pass the huge entrance cave of the old mine workings, on the left, then continues to contour across the fell. At a fork keep ahead above the woods which separate Rydal Water from Grasmere. Soon you are looking down on Grasmere from the high path known as **Loughrigg Terrace**.

3. Immediately before the path enters woods ahead, turn sharp left and follow the path up onto **Loughrigg Fell**. The path—pitched with stones for most of the way—rises steeply onto the fell and gives increasingly wide views back to Rydal Water and Grasmere, and across to Heron Pike. As you climb higher the Langdale Pikes join the expanding list of fells that come into view.

The summit offers stunning views in every direction—from the long arm of Windermere to the south, past the Coniston and Langdale fells, to the looming bulk of Fairfield in the north.

4. From the **summit of Loughrigg Fell**, take the broad path marked by large cairns which heads south-east, towards

Birds' eye view: *The stunning view from Loughrigg Fell to Grasmere and Helm Crag*

Windermere. The route is easily followed as it is the most obvious of the many paths leading all over the fell, and is marked regularly by large stone cairns. At a small saddle with a tiny tarn over to the left, the path swings to the right to avoid a small rounded summit and soon Ambleside comes into view, ahead.

5. Keep to the most obvious path ahead, and descend gently to a low point on the broad ridge, with a tiny pool on the right. Cross the stream here by large stepping stones and begin to rise. The path soon levels (before a small group of conifers ahead); turn right here, onto a much narrower path. Follow this over a small summit then continue ahead with walled fields on you left. Go through a kissing gate in a crossing fence and follow the path parallel to the wall. Walk ahead until you reach a small circular tarn with a single tree on a small island. This is **Lily Tarn**.

6. Keep to the path around the left-hand side of the tarn. At the far end of the tarn, turn left onto a narrow path. It

Loughrigg Terrace: *Walkers enjoy aerial views of Grasmere, Heron Pike and Helm Crag from the elevated path of Loughrigg Terrace*

soon passes a small, marshy pool to reach a kissing gate in a wall, with Ambleside visible below.

Go through the gate and follow the path down to cross a footbridge over the beck and into the woods. The path leads through the trees to an access road. Turn right along the road.

7. At a T-junction, turn right again and, opposite the gates to 'Loughrigg Brow', turn left over a stone footbridge across the **River Rothay**. Immediately after the

bridge, don't follow the path to the right, instead go through the gate directly ahead onto a tarmac footpath. Follow this to a no through road called Stony Lane. Continue to the main A591, on the outskirts of Ambleside.

8. Turn left along the main road, heading away from Ambleside. A few hundred metres later, and immediately after **Scandale Bridge**, turn right through stone gate posts onto the unmetalled road through **Rydal Park**.

Around a kilometre later, the drive enters the wooded grounds of **Rydal Hall**. Continue along the drive and, just before the bridge, turn right, following

the signs. The right of way passes the conference centre, crosses a bridge and goes past tearooms to reach a lane. Turn left down the lane.

At the main road, turn right. Opposite the **Badger Bar** cross over, go through the gate and across the footbridge. Walk up the field and through a small wood to reach the lane. Turn right, and return to the car park to complete the walk. ♦

Ancient boundaries

Drystone walls are an essential feature of the upland landscapes of northern Britain. There are more than 3,000 miles of drystone walls within the Lake District National Park alone. These traditional field boundaries are built without mortar and often date back to the Enclosure Acts of the eighteenth century. Happily, growing recognition of their cultural importance means the future of Cumbria's drystone walls is bright.

Wansfell from the Kirkstone Pass road

Wansfell Pike

Ambleside - Stock Ghyll Park Wood – Wansfell – Nanny Lane – Troutbeck - Skelghyll Woods – Ambleside

What to expect:
Lanes and woodland paths, steep, open fell paths, bridleways

Distance: 9.5km/ 6 miles

Ascent/descent: 335m/1,100 feet

Start: There are several Pay and Display car parks in Ambleside. The walk begins close to Barclays Bank and the Market Hall, in the town centre

Grid ref: NY 376 045

Ordnance Survey Map: OL 7 *The English Lakes South-eastern area. Windermere, Kendal & Silverdale*

Wainwrights: None

Walk outline

From Ambleside, easy walking along lanes and woodland paths lead to Stock Ghyll Force. This is followed by a long, steep climb to the summit of Wansfell Pike. This is a tough climb but the spectacular views make it worthwhile. A more gentle descent over open moors leads to the village of Troutbeck with its two country pubs—a great mid walk break. Return to Ambleside is by Robin Lane, an old, unsurfaced fell road that follows the contours and gives excellent views out over Windermere.

Wansfell Pike

The ascent of Wansfell Pike from Ambleside is a tough climb for such a modest fell, but the magnificent panorama from the summit more than compensates for this. The view takes in almost the full length of Windermere with its wooded islands, a bird's-eye view of Ambleside and most of the central fells—from the Old Man of Coniston out to the west, past the Langdale fells, the Fairfield range and finally the shapely tops of the Kentmere Horseshoe.

Troutbeck village, with its two excellent pubs, makes a perfect mid-walk break, with an easy return to Ambleside.

Take a mid-walk break

Stonechat

The Walk

1. From the centre of **Ambleside**, follow the narrow road between Barclays Bank and the Market Hall. Almost immediately this swings left and begins a gentle climb high above the wooded gill on the left. Look for the path on the left signed to 'Stock Ghyll Force and Stock Ghyll Park Wood'.

2. Follow the path through **Stock Ghyll Park Wood** with the gill down to the left and, at a fork, bear left down steps to cross the gill by a footbridge. The path swings right now, along the left-hand bank. At a fork the right-hand path leads to a viewing area for **Stock Ghyll Force** waterfall.

Double back to the fork and turn sharp right to cross the gill again above the falls by another footbridge. Follow the path to a second viewing area where the path forks. Bear left to shortly exit the woods by an old turnstile gate, back into the lane.

Turn left up the lane, soon passing over a cattle grid. A little further on, look for steps and a stile on the right signed for 'Troutbeck via Wansfell'.

3. Beyond the stile the route follow the obvious, well-made path, which climbs steeply beside a stream on the left. The path takes a direct line, becoming steeper as you ascend, with widening views back to Ambleside and across to the Langdale fells and Fairfield.

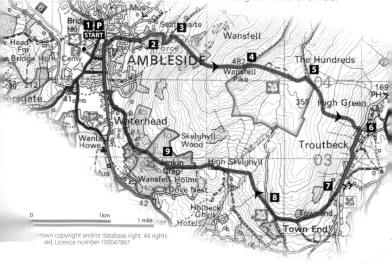

Heavenly light: *Wansfell is overlooked by the giants of Fairfield and Red Screes*

Higher up, the path crosses the stream and continues the ascent, eventually passing through a gap in the stone wall on the left. The path climbs a little more before the final few metres zigzag steeply to the little pointed top. Go through a small gate here, to reach the **summit of Wansfell**.

4. The path continues east from the summit, descending across the open moors. Go through a gate in a crossing wall. Continue through another gate in a crossing wall to enter a track flanked by stone walls, called **Nanny Lane**.

5. Turn right, and follow Nanny Lane down into **Troutbeck** village. The track enters the village beside Lane Foot Farm.

(To visit the pubs in Troutbeck, turn left here into the centre of the village; afterwards retrace your steps to Lane Foot Farm).

6. Turn right out of Nanny Lane, and walk through the village past a series of wells built into the walls on the right. Continue for 800 metres to the village post office, opposite a lane on the left.

Morning mist: *Early morning fog hangs over Windermere*

7. Bear right here, off the road, onto a narrow lane signposted to 'Ambleside'. When the tarmac ends beyond the houses, the lane continues uphill as a stony track between stone walls. It's called **Robin Lane** on some maps. Follow the track as it climbs gradually and swings gently to the right.

8. About 1.5 kilometres from Troutbeck village you reach a gate on the left with a path signed to 'Skelghyll and Ambleside'. Bear left here and follow the path down the edge of two large fields. The views to the left look out across Windermere to the Coniston and Langdale fells. Cross the stream and continue on the obvious path, which soon swings left to join a lane end in the corner of the field.

Turn right along the lane, and follow it through the yard of **High Skelghyll Farm**. Beyond the farm, the path continues ahead to enter **Skelghyll Woods** by a gate. The path drops gently downhill through the woods.

(Within 600 metres there is a National Trust board on the left showing a short detour to the viewpoint at **Jenkin Crag**).

9. Continue on the path through the woods, bearing right at a fork. Cross a stone bridge and walk downhill. Keep right at a junction and walk on to reach a tarmac lane leading into **Ambleside**.

On the outskirts of Ambleside, walk to the main road, then turn right, back to the town centre to complete the walk. ♦

Stock Ghyll Force

Just a short walk from the centre of Ambleside, Stock Ghyll Force is a spectacular 20-metre waterfall surrounded by mature oak woodland. Originally within the grounds of the Salutation Hotel, the falls were popular with Victorian tourists who paid a penny to 'make the safe and easy descent to the foot of the falls'. Contemporary posters also advertised 'Bathing under the falls—towelling provided'. Brrrr!

Wetherlam from the summit of Holme Fell

Holme Fell

Tongue Intake – High Oxen Fell – Hodge Close Quarry – Holme Fell – Uskdale Gap – Tongue Intake

What to expect:
Quiet lanes, woodland paths, open, heather covered fell, rocky paths

Distance: 6.5km/ 4 miles

Ascent/descent: 198m/650 feet

Start: Limited parking at the lane junction at the National Trust's Tongue Intake Plantation, off the A593 Ambleside to Coniston Road

Grid ref: NY 329 022

Ordnance Survey Map: OL 7 *The English Lakes South-eastern area. Windermere, Kendal & Silverdale*

Wainwright summits: Holme Fell

Walk outline

From the parking area near Tongue Intake Plantation, a delightful lane winds its way to the old hill farm of High Oxen Fell. Lakeland tracks then take you through open woods to the impressive Hodge Close Quarry. From here a devious path rises along the north-western flanks of Holme Fell, with its wide views of the Coniston Fells and lake. Return is made via Uskdale Gap and the splendidly wild, but little known, north-east ridge of Holme Fell. The terrain on the open fell is complicated so avoid the walk in poor visibility.

Summit scramble

Holme Fell

Holme Fell rises to just 317 metres, but you get a lot of fell for your money with this tiddler. Often ignored by walkers heading for the higher tops, this fell becomes a favourite of all those who walk its upper reaches. And because it often avoids the worst of the weather on grubby days, it can offer a good fell day when the big boys are out of the question.

The heather-covered summit offers superb views to the higher fells of the Coniston group and out over Coniston Water in clear conditions.

Bell heather

The Walk

1. Roughly 30 metres from the main road beside the National Trust's **Tongue Intake Plantation**, the lane forks. Take the left-hand fork and follow the lane past a bench on the left. The lane crosses a brook then rises steeply to pass between two cottages. Carry on to a lane junction and bear right, signposted to **'High Oxen Fell Farm'**.

Follow the lane to reach the farm at the end of the tarmaced lane. Go through the farmyard and the gate ahead.

2. Beyond the farm, the unsurfaced lane runs through open woods and scrub. It's a byway often used by off-roaders.

Cross a stream and continue uphill through a gate, to reach old quarry workings over to the left. Go through the gate and keep ahead on the track with the quarry workings on your left. (You can detour here to see the first of the quarries; but be especially careful with children as the workings are all unfenced.)

3. When you reach a fork in the lane, turn left and walk on between cottages and outbuildings. The lane rises gently. At the top of the rise, look out for the impressive **Hodge Close Quarry** on the left.

Hodge Close is one of the many quarries in the area around Tilberthwaite, some worked until as recently as the 1960s. It is one of the most impressive, with a depth of over 100 metres (300ft).

Continue along the lane, which is edged with rocks where it crosses an open area. Soon afterwards, the lane enters woods, opposite a large gate on the right.

Turn left here, across the head of the quarry, to reach a gate near a stile and National Trust sign for 'Holme Fell'.

0   1km
                    ½ mile

Woods, tarns and fells. *Looking north from Holme Fell to the distant Langdale Pikes*

4. Cross the stile to reach a T-junction of paths. Turn right, and follow the excellent path through the woods, with a wall on your right. Go through a gate beside a stile and follow the winding path through the woods, with quarry workings up to your left. Continue until you see a row of stone houses across a field on the right. Farther on, around 50 metres before a gate ahead, look for a path cutting sharply to the left, up through the bracken.

5. At the top of the rise, the summit of Holme Fell becomes clear ahead. Continue on the obvious path, aiming a little to the right of the summit, crossing a boggy area and ignoring paths off to the left. Climb steadily between swathes of bracken and heather. Higher up, the path swings left to reach a little col on the broad ridge with a view over Coniston Lake. Take one of the minor footpaths on the left that lead up to the rocky **summit of Holme Fell**, marked by a cairn.

6. Two paths continue beyond the summit. Take the left-hand path and

Quiet lane: *There are superb views to Wetherlam and the Langdale fells from the old lane to High Oxen Fell Farm*

within 30 metres bear right at a second fork. Follow the path down to a broad col curving to the right around a wet area to reach a cairned summit beyond.

From this minor top, the route ahead is clear. Below, look for a small tarn just before woods with a large, broken crag to its right. The route follows a path to the right of the crag, running along the north-east ridge of the fell.

Take one of the paths leading down to the col immediately before the crag (it's

known as **Uskdale Gap**) where there is a cairn and junction of paths.

7. Go straight ahead, on a path to the right of the crag. Follow the ridge path, which undulates between minor tops, then passes between crags in open ground, with broad views to the left.

At a second wet area alongside a fence, bear to the right around the bog, then head left over a rise, to reach a fence corner.

Climb steeply beside the fence. At the top of the slope, turn left over a stile. Follow the path ahead, keeping to the left at a fork. Continue along the

ridge, with a marshy pool down to the right, eventually reaching a wall near overhead power lines.

8. Curve right here, on a path beneath the power lines, to reach a fence corner.

Turn left and go through a gate into a lane. Turn left along the lane, and right at the next junction. Retrace your outward route along the lane to complete the walk. ♦

Cumbria's upland sheep

Sheep and sheep farming have shaped the Cumbrian landscape since time out of mind. Around three million sheep graze the Cumbrian fells today. Hill farms often have 'fell rights' and favour hardy upland breeds that can survive poor grazing and harsh weather. Look out for dark, coarse fleeced Herdwick sheep; large, black-and-white faced Rough Fells; and wiry Swaledales (see left) with their off-white coats and curled horns.

Useful Information

Cumbria Tourism
Cumbria Tourism's official website covers everything from accommodation and events to attractions and adventure. **www.golakes.co.uk**

Lake District National Park
The Lake District National Park website also has information on things to see and do, plus maps, webcams and news. **www.lakedistrict.gov.uk**

Tourist Information Centres
The main TICs provide free information on everything from accommodation and travel to what's on and walking advice.

Ambleside	01539 432 582	tic@thehubofambleside.com
Bowness	01539 442 895	bownesstic@lake-district.gov.uk
Coniston	01539 441 533	mail@conistontic.org
Keswick	01768 772 645	keswicktic@lake-district.gov.uk
Penrith	01768 867 466	pen.tic@eden.gov.uk
Ullswater	01768 482 414	ullswatertic@lake-district.gov.uk
Windermere	01539 446 499	windermeretic@southlakeland.gov.uk

Emergencies
The Lake District is covered by twelve volunteer mountain rescue teams. In a real emergency:

1. Make a note of your location (with OS grid reference, if possible); the name, age and sex of the casualty; their injuries; how many people are in the group; and your mobile phone number.

2. Call 999 or 112 and ask for the Cumbria police, and then for Mountain Rescue.

3. Give them your prepared details.

4. Do NOT change position until contacted by the mountain rescue team.

Weather
Five day forecast for the Lake District: 0844 846 2444
www.lakedistrict.gov.uk/weatherline